CHRIS C

THE SEVEN SPIRITS OF GOD

...divine secrets to the miraculous

LoveWorld Publications

THE SEVEN SPIRITS OF GOD - *divine secrets to the miraculous*

ISBN– 978-37865-0-4

All Scripture quotations are taken from the King James Version of the Bible unless otherwise indicated

BELIEVERS' LOVEWORLD INC.

a.k.a Christ Embassy

UNITED KINGDOM:
Christ Embassy Int'l Office
363 Springfield Road
Chelmsford, Essex, CM2 6AW
Tel:+44 1245 490 234

SOUTH AFRICA:
303 Pretoria Avenue
Cnr. Harley and Hendrik Verwoerd
Randburg, Gauteng
South Africa
Tel: +27-11-326 0971,
+27-11-326 0972

CANADA:
101 RossDean Drive,
Toronto, ON, Canada M9L S6
Tel/Fax:+1-416-746 5080

NIGERIA:
P.O. Box 13563, Ikeja, Lagos.
Tel:+234-8023324188,
+234-8052464131,
+234-1-8925724

USA:
Christ Embassy Int'l Office
2616 Texas Dr A,
Irving, Texas 75062
Tel:+1-972-255-1787

email: cec@christembassy.org
website: www.christembassy.org

Dear Reader,

As you receive the revelations of God in this book, it is my prayer that you will experience the fullness of the Spirit, and that the miraculous and supernatural will become a regular occurrence in your life as the seven Spirits of God have their way and manifest themselves in you. God bless you.

Pastor Chris

Contents

Introduction

When you hear or read the title, "The Seven Spirits of God" for the first time, the first question that will likely come up in your mind is, *Does this mean God has seven Holy Spirits?*

The Bible does show that there are "Seven Spirits of God." It however behooves us to understand exactly what this means and how it applies to us in the New Covenant.

To start with, the number **Seven (7)** is regarded by the Hebrew people as a sacred number, and throughout the Bible it is used to symbolize perfection, fullness, abundance, rest, and completion. The "Seven Spirits of God" therefore implies a "completeness" or "fullness" of the Holy Spirit, and this fullness of the Spirit is what every Christian ought to have, for it is our birthright.

One time, a highly-revered minister (whom I also hold in very high regard) said something many believers have accepted: that only Jesus didn't have the Holy Spirit by measure, but every one of us born again, Spirit-filled believers has the Spirit by measure.

Well, I don't buy that because it's not in the Bible! The reason many Christians have accepted this is that they don't understand the manifestations and capabilities of the Holy Spirit. They figure that the only way He can spread Himself throughout the whole world is to be in Jesus fully and in each of us in smaller measures. The truth, however, is that when you were born again and you received the Holy Ghost, you didn't receive Him in a measure; you received all of Him!

The Spirit Without Measure

When the Spirit of God came upon Moses, Samson, Samuel, David, Isaiah and all of God's prophets, priests, judges, and kings of old, they received the anointing in a measure. But the Bible says of Jesus, *"For he whom God hath sent speaketh the words of God: for God giveth not the Spirit by measure unto him"* (John 3:34). Jesus was the first who didn't have the Spirit of God (or the anointing) by measure but in His fullness.

This same Jesus, Who had the fullness of God's Spirit, said to His disciples just before He ascended into heaven, *"...as my Father hath sent me, even so send I you"* (John 20:21). Now think about it: If Jesus required the full measure of the Spirit to do the work the Father sent Him, and He has sent us the same way He was sent of the Father, why then should we be sent with a measure and not the fullness of the Spirit?

Moreover, Jesus said in John 14:12, *"Truly, truly, I say to you, he who believes in Me, the works that I do, he will do also; and greater {works} than these he will do; because I go to the Father"* (NASB).

How shall we do the same works that Jesus did, and even greater works, if all we have is a measure of the Spirit He had while He was here on earth?

But thank God, we are joint-heirs with Christ Jesus (Romans 8:17). That means we have the same anointing that Jesus had. The whole Holy Ghost, not a part or a measure of Him, is in us, praise God! Through this book, I seek not only to stir in you a strong desire for this fullness of the Spirit, but also to impart to you the revelation knowledge you require to activate it in your life.

It's my strong belief and sincere prayer that through the teachings and revelations that will come to your spirit as you read this book, you'll discover a new and deeper dimension of the Holy Ghost. You'll be able to operate in His fullness always, and you'll walk in the miraculous and the supernatural consistently.

1

THE SEVEN SPIRITS

And there shall come forth a rod out of the stem of Jesse, and a Branch shall grow out of his roots: And the spirit of the Lord shall rest upon him, the spirit of wisdom and understanding, the spirit of counsel and might, the spirit of knowledge and of the fear of the Lord; And shall make him of quick understanding in the fear of the Lord: and he shall not judge after the sight of his eyes, neither reprove after the hearing of his ears: But with righteousness shall he judge the poor, and reprove with

equity for the meek of the earth..."

(Isaiah 11:1-4).

Jesus is the Rod that Isaiah prophesied would come from the stem of Jesse. Jesse was the father of David, and Jesus described Himself as the root and the offspring of David (Revelations 22:16). That's because He's the Root from which David came forth, but He also came to earth physically from David's lineage as his offspring. That's why He was severally addressed in the synoptic gospels as the Son of David.

Isaiah prophesied concerning Him and said when He comes, He would be so full of the Holy Ghost, Who would make Him of quick understanding in the fear of the Lord. As a result, He would not judge according to His sight, neither would He reprove after the hearing of His ears, but would judge the poor and the meek with righteousness and equity (Isaiah 11:3-4).

However, what I really want you to observe is the description Isaiah gives of the Spirit upon Jesus:

"And the spirit of the Lord shall rest upon him, the spirit of wisdom and understanding, the spirit of counsel and might, the spirit of knowledge and of the fear of the Lord;"

(Isaiah 11:2).

This is teaching us something special about the Holy Ghost. If you speed-read through this portion of Scripture without studying it carefully, you won't understand it. But by revelation, you can see God showing us through this and several other Scriptures that there are indeed ***seven Spirits of God.***

The Scriptures, in several places, speak of the Spirit as *the seven eyes, the seven Spirits,* or *the seven lamps.* These we would see shortly.

SEVEN INDEPENDENT MANIFESTATIONS OF THE SPIRIT

In **Isaiah 11:2**, seven distinct 'Spirits' are mentioned. These are:

- *The Spirit of the Lord*
- *The Spirit of Wisdom*
- *The Spirit of Understanding*
- *The Spirit of Counsel*
- *The Spirit of Might*
- *The Spirit of Knowledge*
- *The Spirit of the Fear of the Lord*

All of these seven Spirits are really one Holy Spirit in different manifestations. The same term, "seven Spirits" is also used to portray Him in **Revelation 1:4, Revelation 4:5,** and **Revelation 5:6.**

Revelation 1:4:

"John to the seven churches which are in Asia: Grace be unto you, and peace, from him which is, and which was, and which is to come; and from the seven Spirits which are before his throne;"

Revelation 4:5:

"And out of the throne proceeded lightnings and thunderings and voices: and there were seven lamps of fire burning before the throne, which are the seven Spirits of God."

Revelation 5:6:

"And I beheld, and, lo, in the midst of the throne and of the four beasts, and in the midst of the elders, stood a Lamb as it had been slain, having seven horns and seven eyes, which are the seven Spirits of God sent forth into all the earth."

The seven Spirits of God refer to seven independent manifestations of the Holy Spirit. This is, however, not the same as when we say the Godhead is made up of three Persons. The Trinity is a different phenomenon altogether. Each member of the Godhead—Father, Son, and Holy

Spirit—is a distinct personality with peculiar characteristics and attributes.

In the seven Spirits of God, we're dealing with one Person (the Holy Spirit) and the seven ways in which He operates and manifests Himself. We're talking about "the sevenfold Holy Spirit of God." You'll find this term in *The Amplified Bible* translation of **Revelation 1:4:**

> **"John to the seven assemblies (churches) that are in Asia: May grace (God's unmerited favor) be granted to you and spiritual peace (the peace of Christ's kingdom) from Him Who is and Who was and Who is to come, and from the seven Spirits [the sevenfold Holy Spirit] before His throne,"**

This verse is quite striking. It's not talking about seven separate personalities, but seven separate and independent manifestations of the Holy Spirit in the life of the believer, which is indicative of the fullness of the Spirit.

Isaiah's prophetic words about these seven Spirits of God may not be immediately understood until you read other portions of the Bible. Zechariah, another Old Testament prophet, helps shed more light on "the seven Spirits."

> **"For behold the stone that I have laid before Joshua; upon one stone shall be seven eyes: behold, I will engrave the graving thereof, saith the Lord of hosts, and I will remove the iniquity of that land in one day"**
>
> **(Zechariah 3:9).**

Keep in mind what Zechariah says here that **"Upon one stone shall be seven eyes."**

> **Zechariah 4:10:**
> **"For who hath despised the day of small things? for they shall rejoice, and shall see the plummet in the hand of Zerubbabel with those seven; they are the eyes of the Lord, which run to and fro through the whole earth."**

He said upon one stone shall be seven eyes. Here, in verse 10 of chapter 4, Zechariah refers to those seven eyes upon one stone as the eyes of the Lord, which run to and fro throughout the whole earth.

> **Revelation 5:6:**
> **"And I beheld, and, lo, in the midst of the throne and of the four beasts, and in the midst of the elders, stood a Lamb as it had been slain, having seven horns and seven eyes, which are the seven Spirits of God sent forth into all the earth."**

All three portions of Scripture quoted above speak of one thing—the seven Spirits of God, or put otherwise, the sevenfold Holy Ghost and His operations.

Revelation 1:4 and **Revelation 4:5** tell us more about this:

> **"John, to the seven churches which are in Asia: Grace to you and peace from Him who is and who was and who is to come,**

and from the seven Spirits who are before His throne..."

"And out of the throne proceeded lightnings and thunderings and voices: and there were seven lamps of fire burning before the throne, which are the seven Spirits of God."

There it is again: "The seven Spirits." Remember that Zechariah prophesied that upon one stone shall be seven eyes. The Stone he was talking about was the same one he referred to as the Branch in Zechariah 3:8 and Zechariah 6:12. Isaiah also called Him the Branch (Isaiah 11:1). This means the Branch is the same One called the Stone, which is the Christ.

Over in the New Testament, Peter calls Him "the Living Stone" and "the Chief Cornerstone."

1 Peter 2:3-6:
"If so be ye have tasted that the Lord is gracious. To whom coming, as unto a living stone, disallowed indeed of men,

but chosen of God, and precious, Ye also, as lively stones, are built up a spiritual house, an holy priesthood, to offer up spiritual sacrifices, acceptable to God by Jesus Christ. Wherefore also it is contained in the scripture, Behold, I lay in Sion a chief corner stone, elect, precious: and he that believeth on him shall not be confounded."

Jesus is the Stone, and we also are living stones formed from and fashioned after Him. Observe again what Zechariah said: "Upon one stone shall be seven eyes." Notice he didn't say, "Upon *the* stone" but "upon *one* stone," meaning there are other stones, and upon each of the stones will be seven eyes.

Peter also said He (Jesus) is the Chief Cornerstone and we also are living stones. Each of us in His presence is a stone.

Again, remember that He is called the Branch, and He said, "I am the Vine, and ye are the branches." That's talking about us. We're the branches of the Branch; we're living stones and upon each of us should be seven eyes, which are the seven Spirits of God.

Why The Seven Spirits?

When the Bible talks about the Holy Ghost as the seven Spirits of God, what it implies is the fullness of the Spirit, which you may or may not have in your life.

In **Ephesians 5:18**, Paul charges us, **"Be not drunk with wine wherein is excess but be filled with the Spirit."** The mere fact that he instructs us to be filled with the Spirit presupposes that we're not always filled with the Spirit. If we were, he would have said, "For ye are filled with the Spirit."

When the Holy Ghost comes to live in you, He'll always be in you. Jesus said He'll abide with you forever (John 14:16), but that's not to say you'll always have His fullness. **When you have less than the seven Spirits of God manifested in you, it means you don't have the fullness of the Spirit.** However, God wants us always to be filled with the Spirit. He wants us to have the fullness of the Spirit in us, and we can, because it belongs to us!

John 3:34 tells us Jesus received the Spirit without measure, which means all seven Spirits of God dwelt in Him. He had the fullness of the Godhead dwelling in Him bodily, and Paul lets us know we are complete in Him Who is the Head of all principality and power (Colossians 2:9-10).

Thus, every child of God ought to have the fullness of the Spirit. None of us should have the Spirit with measure. When Paul charged us to "be filled with the Spirit," he was talking about this completeness or fullness of the Spirit.

Revelation 5:6 declares that all seven Spirits of God have been sent forth into all the earth. This means every Christian who has received the Holy Spirit actually has these seven Spirits of God dwelling in him, more so because Zechariah prophesied that upon each stone shall be seven eyes and these seven eyes are the seven Spirits of God.

However, to receive the Spirit, and to have Him fully manifested in your life are two different things altogether. It's great to know that we can have these seven Spirits, but more importantly, we need to know what they do for us and how to walk in them. That's because until the Lord manifests Himself in your life fully through these seven Spirits, you'll never enjoy the best of Christianity, which is the life of the supernatural and the miraculous.

2

THE SPIRIT OF THE LORD

"**And the spirit of the Lord shall rest upon him..."**

(Isaiah 11:2).

The first of the seven Spirits mentioned by the prophet Isaiah is the **Spirit of the Lord**. This is also known as the **Spirit of Lordship** or the **Spirit of dominion**.

THE ONE WHO "COMES UPON"

Many Christians know little or nothing about this Spirit. He's the One Who always "rests upon" or "comes upon." He's the One Who anoints you with power for service. Every time you find Him described in both the Old and New Testaments, He always "comes upon."

The Spirit of the Lord gives you boldness and the sense of dominion. He puts you in charge of situations. This was what the prophets of old needed whenever they stood to declare God's Word before kings whom they would ordinarily have been afraid of. Whenever they needed boldness to dominate their circumstances or to speak God's Word without fear or timidity, the Spirit of the Lord came upon them and empowered them.

Often, you'll read concerning the prophets, "And the Spirit of the Lord was upon him." That was the Spirit of Lordship in operation. He took charge and the one before whom they stood could do nothing against them.

He's the reason Elijah could go around looking for the notoriously wicked King Ahab to deliver God's message of judgment to him. Ahab, on seeing Elijah, exclaimed, "Have you found me, oh my enemy!"(1 Kings 21:20), and Elijah replied, "Yes, I've found you, for you are the enemy of Israel. You have sold yourself to work evil in the sight of the Lord!" (1 Kings 21:20). Elijah could speak with such boldness because he was inspired by the Spirit of the Lord.

When God called Moses and sent him to Pharaoh with the message: "Let my people go!" he didn't think he could do it, and he started giving God excuses. But God's grace prevailed and the Spirit of the Lord came upon him. It wasn't the signs God showed Moses that gave him boldness to go before Pharaoh as much as the Spirit of the Lord that came upon him.

When he got to Pharaoh's palace, he said, "Thus saith the Lord God of Israel, Let My people go!"

Pharaoh sneered, "Who is your God?" But that was the worst he could do. He couldn't order Moses' summary execution, which normally would have been his immediate response to such effrontery. Moses was moved to challenge him by the Spirit of the Lord.

When Joshua was about to take over the reins of leadership of Israel from Moses, it was the Spirit of the Lord Who assured him and said, *"No one will be able to oppose you as long as you live, for I will be with you just as I was with Moses; I will not abandon you or fail to help you"* (Joshua 1:5 TLB).

He also told him, *"Have I not commanded you? Be strong and of good courage; do not be afraid, nor be dismayed, for the* L*ORD your God is with you wherever you go"* (Joshua 1:9 NKJV).

He said to Paul, *"Don't be afraid! Speak out! Don't quit! For I am with you and no one can harm you. Many people here in this city belong to me"* (Acts 18:9-10 TLB). This emboldened Paul and he *"...stayed there the next year and a half, teaching the truths of God"* (Acts 18:11).

In the Old Testament, the Spirit of the Lord came upon a young prophet named Azariah, and he prophesied God's Word to the king and the entire nation:

"And the Spirit of God came upon Azariah the son of Oded: And he went out to meet Asa, and said unto him, Hear ye me, Asa, and all Judah and Benjamin; The Lord is with you, while ye be with him; and if ye seek him, he will be found of you; but if ye forsake him, he will forsake you"

(2 Chronicles 15:1-2).

Azariah and many other prophets stood before kings and rulers and spoke boldly to them because the Spirit of the Lord came upon them. In the New Covenant, Paul tells us **"God hath not given us the spirit of fear (or timidity); but of power, and of love, and of a sound mind" (2 Timothy 1:7).**

If you've received the Holy Spirit to live in you, you're no longer ordinary. You have the boldness of God in you to do anything that is consistent with His will. That's what we've got, but many of us haven't understood or taken advantage of this, because we haven't really walked with the Spirit of the Lord as we should.

THE OPERATIONS OF THE SPIRIT OF THE LORD

There's a special anointing the Spirit of the Lord brings with Him. We see this anointing in operation when He visits prophet Ezekiel:

> **"...This was the appearance of the likeness of the glory of the LORD. And when I saw it, I fell upon my face, and I heard a voice of one that spake"**
>
> **(Ezekiel 1:28).**

Ezekiel saw the glory of the Lord and he fell flat on his face, completely overwhelmed by His awesome presence. Now watch what happens next:

> **"And he said unto me, Son of man, stand upon thy feet, and I will speak unto thee. And the spirit entered into me when he spake unto me, and set me upon my feet, that I heard him that spake unto me"**
>
> **(Ezekiel 2:1-2).**

The Lord said, "Get up on your feet, I want to talk to you," and Ezekiel recounted that when He said that, the Spirit entered him and set him on his feet.

This is a special operation of the Spirit of the Lord. He wasn't with Ezekiel before this time, but when He came, He entered him from the outside and set him upon his feet. He does that for us from time to time.

Have you ever been in a state where you thought you were just too weak and tired to pray? Still you made an attempt to mumble a few words of prayer: "Father, I thank You for this day. Thank You in Jesus' Name..." and you spoke in tongues a little. Then you heard the Spirit say, "Get up and pray!" It sounded rather authoritative, but you thought to yourself, "God understands I'm really tired," and continued mumbling weakly in tongues. But the next thing you knew, you were wide awake, pacing the floor, speaking so powerfully in other tongues, and you didn't have a clue how it happened.

That was the Spirit of the Lord at work. He entered you and set you upon your feet, just as He did Ezekiel!

You see, it's because we don't recognize these operations of the Spirit and feel we're the ones doing them by ourselves that the Spirit of God doesn't do much more in our lives. All the time, we give ourselves the credit and say, "I was very tired when I started praying, but suddenly I just felt like getting up to pray and I got up and started praying." We fail to acknowledge the Spirit.

Ezekiel was smarter than that. He knew he couldn't have gotten up by himself because he was knocked flat out. He recognized it was the Spirit of the Lord Who entered him and set him upon his feet and made him alert so he could hear the words of the Lord. Glory to God!

In chapter 3 and verse 12, Ezekiel said, *"Then the spirit **took me up**, and I heard behind me a voice of a great rushing, saying, Blessed be the glory of the Lord from his place."* But notice that it wasn't mentioned anywhere before this that the Spirit went out of him after He entered him in Ezekiel 2:2. He hadn't gone out of him, yet He took him up again in Ezekiel 3:12.

There's another interesting operation of the Spirit in verse 14:

> **"So the spirit lifted me up, and took me away, and I went in bitterness, in the heat of my spirit; but the hand of the Lord was strong upon me"**
>
> **(Ezekiel 3:14).**

Ezekiel said the Spirit lifted him up and took him away. That's got to be an outside force! The same Spirit of the Lord that entered into Ezekiel was still ministering to him from the outside.

A similar event is recorded in the New Testament in **Acts 8:39:**

> **"And when they were come up out of the water, the Spirit of the Lord caught away Philip, that the eunuch saw him no more: and he went on his way rejoicing."**

Every time you find the rendering *"the Spirit of the Lord"* in the New Testament, pay close attention to it. It didn't just say here that "the Spirit caught away Philip," but "the **Spirit of the Lord** caught away Philip." Remember, Philip was born again and had the Holy Ghost in him. But this was another function of the Holy Spirit coming from outside him.

"The Spirit of the Lord caught away Philip..." That had to have happened from the outside. He carried Philip away physically and took him somewhere else (Acts 8:40). Now, that's some power! And that's the Spirit the Lord was talking about when He said, *"Ye shall receive power, after that the Holy Ghost is come upon you..."* (Acts1:8).

The Spirit of The Lord Empowers You

Jesus told His disciples, *"ye shall receive power, after that the Holy Ghost is come upon you: and ye shall be witnesses unto me both in Jerusalem, and in all Judaea, and in Samaria, and unto the uttermost part of the earth"* (Acts 1:8). But before this time, He had told them to wait in the city of Jerusalem until they were endued with power from on high (Luke 24:49).

On the day of Pentecost, when the Holy Ghost came upon them, they received and were endued (clothed) with supernatural power to preach and teach the Word of God. When that happened, they went out and began to speak, knowing that the Holy Spirit would impregnate their words with power to save those who heard them.

Peter knew that power had come. That was why he could tell the man at the Beautiful Gate, *"Silver and gold have I none; but such as I have give I thee: In the name of Jesus Christ of Nazareth rise up and walk"* (Acts 3:6), and when the man didn't respond, he grabbed him by the hand and lifted him up. Then his ankle bones received strength and he began to walk. Peter knew he had power; he knew the Spirit of the Lord was upon him.

Let me remind you that the same Spirit that was upon Jesus, the Chief Cornerstone, is upon each one of us living stones. Jesus said in **Luke 4:18-19**,

> **"The Spirit of the Lord is upon me, because he hath anointed me to preach the gospel to the poor; he hath sent me to heal the brokenhearted, to preach deliverance to the captives, and recovering of sight to the blind, to set at liberty them that are bruised, To preach the acceptable year of the Lord."**

Did you catch the point of this? It means that when the Spirit of the Lord comes upon you, He anoints you to tell the good news. And when you tell it, it doesn't come to your hearers as mere words but with the divine power and ability to give life.

GET SOME POWER!

Some Christians only know to read their Bibles, teach, preach, sing, pray, and go their way. They're in the "meek and quiet" camp. Child of God, there's more to your life than that. You've got to have some power in your life! The Bible says the Kingdom of God is not in Word only, but in power also (1 Corinthians 4:20).

There's nothing as uninspiring as a Christian who preaches power without demonstrating it. Paul said, "I didn't come with words of man's wisdom, but in the demonstration of the Spirit and of power; that your faith shouldn't stand in the wisdom of men but in the power of God" (1 Corinthians 2:4). Therefore, get some power; get to know the Spirit of the Lord!

Many times before I minister, I wait for the anointing of the Spirit of the Lord to come on me. When it does, I know more than anybody else that something has happened. Sometimes, when I'm praying alone, I can tell like Ezekiel, that the Spirit of the Lord just entered me. It feels as if His hands and legs have just gone into mine. I can tell it's not just me moving anymore, but "Someone" moving in me. I can tell that He wants to lay hands through me and do mighty things through me. Glory to God!

The Spirit of The Lord Deals With The Storm

I was preaching at a crusade sometime in 1985, and that was one of the first times I began to observe this manifestation of the Spirit. A strong wind began to blow and it looked like the heavens were about to come down. The place was sandy, so the wind raised so much dust and sand and brought it against the people.

I was grieved in my spirit all the time this was happening. You know, sometimes you can be grieved in your spirit about something but you can't do anything about it yet, because you don't want to do something dumb. I kept thinking to myself, *What's going on? What am I going to do about this?*

Some people were trying to shield themselves from the billowing dust. Others started going away because it was so cloudy. It was obvious there was going to be a heavy downpour. By this time my jacket was already flying in the wind, but I kept on preaching and many tried to listen.

Then suddenly, that unction came and I uttered some words. I only remember that the people started clapping but I didn't know what I said until I later heard it on the tape. I said "Wind, not this way. Turn around and go that way!" When I spoke those words, I saw the wind turn 180 degrees and go in the other direction. Calm returned, the people were able to receive the message, and we had a glorious meeting.

Miracles Happen By the Spirit of the Lord

I remember another incident in 1986. I was preaching at a meeting and there was this crippled young man sitting in the front row with his crutches beside him. I had just started preaching and hadn't quite gone ten minutes into my message when, suddenly, I was full of the Spirit.

I hadn't planned to do this, and I hadn't even thought about it, but right in the middle of my message, I turned abruptly to that crippled fellow, got hold of him and said, "Walk, in Jesus' Name!" I pulled him up, and he started walking! Of course, everybody was shouting, rejoicing and praising God to the high heavens. We went on that night and had more miracles and manifestations of the Spirit.

That's what happens when the Spirit of the Lord takes over. You don't think about it. You don't reason it out and wonder, *What am I going to do now?* He just moves you to act.

When He caught Philip away, He didn't wait for him to prepare specially for it. Philip didn't have the time to announce to the eunuch who was with him, "Now I'm about to journey to Azotus. Nobody knows I'm going there, but I know I am!" No, he wasn't squeezing out faith. The Spirit of the Lord just caught him and took him away.

He's Not A Still, Small Voice

When the Spirit of the Lord comes upon you, you may not be talking but you'll start seeing things. There'll be a new boldness in your soul. That's what the prophet Micah meant when he said, *"I am full of power by the spirit of the Lord, and of judgment, and of might, to declare unto Jacob his transgression, and to Israel his sin"* (Micah 3:8).

Some think of the Spirit of the Lord as "a still, small voice." That's because they don't know Him. He's not a still, small voice; He's the Spirit of dominion.

He welled up in Paul when Elymas the sorcerer challenged him, and the Bible tells us that *"Paul, filled with the Holy Spirit* (the Spirit of the Lord), *glared angrily at the sorcerer and said, You son of the devil, full of every sort of trickery and villainy, enemy of all that is good, will you never end your opposition to the Lord? And now God has laid his hand of punishment upon you, and you will be stricken awhile with blindness. Instantly mist and darkness fell upon him, and he began wandering around begging for someone to take his hand and lead him"* (Acts 13:8-11 TLB).

Now that doesn't sound like a still, small voice, does it?

Prepare Yourself For Him

Some say when you pray hard enough that's when the power comes. No, it's got nothing to do with praying hard but everything to do with your hunger. You see, the Holy Spirit doesn't force Himself on anybody. The question is: How much do you want Him?

If you want Him, He will fill you. He never goes where He's not wanted, except when He shows up to enforce a change or bring judgment. Remember, He's Boss, so we don't stir Him up. We don't shake Him up to get Him to do things. Instead we prepare for Him. The Bible says if you're a vessel that's prepared, you'll be ready and fit for the Master's use (2 Timothy 2:21).

God wants to use you, but He wants you to be ready for Him. He wants you to be cleansed, separated, and sanctified. Then you'll be ready for Him to use you.

3

THE SPIRIT OF WISDOM

"And the spirit of the Lord shall rest upon him, the spirit of wisdom..." (Isaiah 11:2).

The Spirit of wisdom is the One Who brings you the wisdom of God. Paul prayed for the Ephesian Christians *"that the God of our Lord Jesus Christ, the Father of glory, may give unto you the spirit of wisdom and revelation in the knowledge of him:"* (Ephesians 1:17), because he observed that the Ephesian Christians were demonstrating the power and glory of God, but lacked wisdom and revelation knowledge.

This is what happens to a lot of God's people. They have the gifts of the Spirit; they can prophesy and have great things happen, but when it comes to walking in the wisdom and knowledge of the things of God, they're found wanting. Such people need to pray that God will grant them the Spirit of wisdom and revelation in the knowledge of Him. Then they'll be balanced.

To appreciate the work of the Spirit of wisdom, we must first understand what wisdom is. You may not find these definitions in any English dictionary because true wisdom can only be defined by the Spirit of God.

The Accurate Definition of Wisdom

Wisdom is so often defined as the ability to apply knowledge. This definition is inadequate and is usually employed by those who don't understand what real wisdom is. However, when you have the Spirit of wisdom functioning in you, you'd understand how to define wisdom.

Firstly, **Wisdom is a force. It's the divine insight into the plans and purposes of God. It's understanding spiritual realities.**

Wisdom can also be defined as the insight of knowledge and the controlling power of insight. Wisdom is insight into reality (truth), foresight into the future. It causes you to understand what others can't see. With wisdom, you can rightly judge what others can't figure out.

I said wisdom is a force; it's more than an ability. You can have the ability to do something and not do it. For example, you're looking at a glass and you know you're supposed to remove it from where it is. You also know you have the ability to do so, but you don't do it. That's not wisdom. Wisdom causes you to do what you should do!

If you have the ability to apply knowledge and you don't apply it, or you know what's right to do and you don't do it, you're not wise. In fact, you'll be described as a fool, because you knew what to do and how to do it but you still didn't do it!

The wisdom of God has the power to cause you to say what you should say, do what you should do and think what you should think. It makes you go where you should go. Wisdom is not passive; it's manifested by action.

When Paul said, *"For it is God which worketh in you both to will and **to do** of his good pleasure,"* he was talking about the Spirit of wisdom working in us. Wisdom is **the controlling power** that works in us, not just to will, but also **to do** God's good pleasure. It's a force that propels, compels, moves, and motivates. It brings you understanding, information, insight, and knowledge. Wisdom is all-encompassing.

Here's what Wisdom has to say of Himself:

> **"I wisdom dwell with prudence, and find out knowledge of witty inventions"**
>
> **(Proverbs 8:12).**

Wisdom says, "I don't go alone, I have prudence (discretion or good judgment in practical affairs) and knowledge with me." You have insight and foresight because the Spirit of wisdom brings them to you. But His ministry doesn't stop there; He lets loose within your system that controlling force that causes you to act wisely.

With Wisdom, You Have It Made!

When you lack wisdom, you may think the wrong thoughts, say the wrong words, do the wrong things, and make the wrong choices. And most of the problems people have are caused by the wrong choices they made.

Leaders make the wrong choices because they lack wisdom, and as a result nations are thrown into turmoil. People make wrong investments and lose money because they don't have the wisdom of God. Someone marries the wrong person and gets stuck in an unsavoury marriage because he or she lacks wisdom. But when Wisdom resides in you, it will pilot you in the right direction. That's why you need the Spirit of wisdom operating in your life.

When the Spirit of wisdom functions in you, life becomes bright and exciting. In Proverbs 3:13-14, Solomon—the wisest man to live before Jesus—said, *"Happy is the man that findeth wisdom and the man that getteth understanding. For the merchandise of it is better than the merchandise of silver and the gain thereof than fine gold."*

This is the secret! If you find wisdom, you have it made. You cannot fail or be poor, no, not with wisdom!

> **"She (wisdom) is more precious than rubies: and all the things thou canst desire are not to be compared unto her. Length of days is in her right hand; and in her left hand riches and honour. Her ways are ways of pleasantness, and all her paths are peace"**
>
> **(Proverbs 3:15-17).**

When wisdom is working in you, your life will be full of peace. You won't ever have to worry about lack, want, sickness, disease, or anything contrary to the good life. The Hebrew word translated "peace" is "*shalom*." Shalom doesn't just depict quietness and tranquility or an environment where no one is disturbing you. More importantly, shalom means peace with prosperity; peace with everything going on perfectly and under your control.

Shalom is a state of completeness, wholeness, total well-being, health and prosperity that produces rest. Thus, shalom is the peace of God that gives prosperity, health, strength, and advantage.

When you have such peace, you'll sleep like a baby. You won't sleep fitfully and you won't need pills to knock you off to sleep every night. When I sleep, I sleep well! When I laugh, I laugh heartily, not like someone who's trying to. I live a tremendous life because of the peace that wisdom brings.

Christ Is Our Wisdom

"But of him (God) are ye in Christ Jesus, who of God is made unto us wisdom, and righteousness, and sanctification, and redemption:"

(1 Corinthians 1:30).

In the New Testament, we have something that Solomon, in all his wisdom, didn't have—Christ! He's our wisdom. Colossians 2:3 tells us *"In whom (Christ) are hid all the treasures of wisdom and knowledge."* In Christ are hidden all the treasures of wisdom and knowledge. In other words, He is the embodiment of all wisdom and all knowledge.

So when you make Jesus the Lord of your life and He takes up His abode in the quarters of your heart, that's Wisdom dwelling in your heart. However, it's one thing to have Jesus Christ as your Saviour and Lord in general but it's something totally different when He becomes Lord of your mind (your decisions, thoughts, and emotions).

That's when wisdom starts functioning in you.

When Jesus becomes Lord of your mind, He begins to direct your thinking. Your mind becomes anointed of God, and an anointed mind receives sanctified thoughts, thoughts that are reserved for kings. Glory to God!

The Bible says in Proverbs 25:2 that *"It is the glory of God to conceal a thing: but the honour of kings is to search out a matter."* This is what the Bible calls the knowledge of the holy. God hides it from the world, then He ministers divine wisdom to your mind by the anointing of the Holy Ghost and you begin to discover secret things.

Wisdom Can Be Seen and Heard

> **"And the spirit of the LORD shall rest upon him, the spirit of wisdom ...And shall make him of quick understanding in the fear of the LORD: and he shall not judge after the sight of his eyes, neither reprove**

after the hearing of his ears..."

(Isaiah 11:2-3).

Until someone speaks or acts, you may not know he has the Spirit of wisdom, but Wisdom can be seen and heard. When He functioned in Solomon, everybody knew. One day, they brought before him two women who lived in the same house. Both of them had just delivered their babies three days apart from each other. One night, one of them slept over her son and killed him. On realizing she had accidentally killed her baby, she went over to her neighbour's bed and switched the babies.

The other woman woke up the next morning to feed her baby, only to discover he was dead. She looked closely at the dead child and knew he wasn't hers. So she went looking for her baby and saw him with her roommate and tried to claim her child back, but a fight ensued.

When the matter was brought before King Solomon, everyone wondered what he would do about it. None of the women came with their husbands, so no daddy could speak. No one else lived in the house with them, so there were no witnesses.

The king wisely requested for a sword and ordered that the live baby be divided into two. The mother cried out "No! Don't kill him. Give her the baby instead." But the other woman said, "Yes, kill him so he won't belong to either of us." Solomon then stood up and said to the real mother, "This is your baby. Take him."

The Bible says, *"all Israel heard of the judgment which the king had judged; and they feared the king: for they saw that the wisdom of God was in him, to do judgment"* (1 Kings 3:28). I told you wisdom can be seen and heard.

Let Wisdom Take Charge of You

Solomon knew the real mother wouldn't want her child killed. The false mother said, "Go ahead and kill him, so neither of us will have him." That's just like some people who say, "I cannot please you and displease myself." If you're a Christian, you shouldn't talk like that.

Maybe you want to buy a pair of shoes and another person wants to buy the same shoes, then an argument starts. You say, "I picked them first!" But the other fellow insists, "No, I got here *first*."

Just let it go, child of God. Your heavenly Father will get you another one that's even better than that!

Some people still say things like, "If not for God, I know what I'd have done to you," or "If you provoke me, I'll show you the side of me that is not born again." You don't have to say such things, you're a Christian. Let the Spirit of wisdom take charge of your mind, your thoughts, your words and your actions.

Remember, Christ—the embodiment of wisdom—dwells in you and has imparted His nature of wisdom to you. That Spirit of wisdom Paul talked about in Ephesians 1:17 dwells in you. You can begin to take full advantage of His ministry in your life today and live the good life God has planned for you to live.

4

THE SPIRIT OF UNDERSTANDING

"That the God of our Lord Jesus Christ, the Father of glory, may give unto you the spirit of wisdom and revelation in the knowledge of him: The eyes of your understanding being enlightened; that ye may know what is the hope of his calling, and what the riches of the glory of his inheritance in the saints"

(Ephesians 1:17-18).

Observe the content of Paul's prayer for the Ephesian saints in verse 18: *"The eyes of your understanding being enlightened."* This is an operation of the Spirit of understanding. He's the One Who helps you understand the hope to which you've been called by God and the wealth of His glorious inheritance in you.

Paul also prayed for them in Ephesians 3:18-19 that they *"May be able to* ***comprehend*** *(that is, understand) with all saints what is the breadth, and length, and depth, and height; And to know the love of Christ, which passeth knowledge...."*

This prayer of Paul the apostle for the Ephesian Christians to understand and know together with all saints the breadth, and length, and depth, and height of the love of Christ was necessary because they had not yet understood or known the depth and power of the love of Christ. They didn't have in demonstration the Spirit of understanding and the Spirit of knowledge.

Today, there are those who may have the gifts of the Spirit in manifestation but lack understanding of the Word. Such people need to pray that they will be filled with the Spirit of understanding so they can understand together with other saints the power of Christ's love for them and in them.

Jesus Imparted the Spirit of Understanding to His Disciples

The anointing of the Spirit comes on us at different times and in different ways, but we need to understand the Spirit's purpose. Anybody can study the Bible, however only when you're anointed can you understand God's Word and receive revelations of the Spirit. The anointing can come on you to give you understanding of the Word. Such an anointing comes from the Spirit of understanding.

John the apostle writes: *"Then said Jesus to them again, Peace be unto you: as my Father hath sent me, even so send I you. And when he had said this, he breathed on them, and saith unto them, Receive ye the Holy Ghost:"* (John 20:21-22).

Jesus was talking to His disciples and He breathed on them. The word translated "breathed" here is "emphusao" which also means "to blow at or on." So Jesus *blew* on them and said unto them, "Receive ye the Holy Ghost!"

I want you to know this was not the same occasion as when the Holy Ghost came to dwell in them, because we read later in Acts 2:1-4 that the same disciples on the day of Pentecost, were all together in one place, in one accord, and they were all filled with the Holy Ghost and began to speak with other tongues.

John's record of the event in John 20:22 helps give an explanation to the account of Luke in **Luke 24:45:**

> **"Then opened he their understanding, that they might understand the scriptures,"**

John lets us know how Jesus opened their hearts and imparted understanding to them.

Understand that the synoptic gospels are Matthew, Mark and Luke. John's gospel was written long after these first three and the reason he wrote it was to clarify what many regard as the dark areas in the synoptic gospels.

So we get the clearest picture of what happened when we put John 20:22 and Luke 24:45 together. We see that when Jesus blew on His disciples and said to them, "Receive ye the Holy Ghost," He actually imparted the Spirit of understanding to them and their minds were anointed to understand the Scriptures.

With All Your Getting, Get Understanding!

Solomon said, *"Wisdom is the principal thing; therefore get wisdom: and* ***with all thy getting get understanding****"* (Proverbs 4:7). You'll see why understanding is so important when you read the parable of the sower in Mark chapter 4:

> **"Hearken; Behold, there went out a sower to sow: And it came to pass, as he sowed, some fell by the way side, and the fowls of the air came and devoured it up...The**

sower soweth the word. And these are they by the way side, where the word is sown; but when they have heard, Satan cometh immediately, and taketh away the word that was sown in their hearts"

(Mark 4:3-4,14-15).

While explaining this parable to His disciples, Jesus revealed to them that the seeds that fell by the wayside represented those who heard the Word of God and didn't understand it, and because they didn't understand it, the devil came immediately and stole the Word from their hearts.

"When any one heareth the word of the kingdom, and understandeth it not, then cometh the wicked one, and catcheth away that which was sown in his heart. This is he which received seed by the way side"

(Matthew 13:19).

The first time I read this scripture, I was amazed that Satan could steal the Word of God, but he did—from the hearts of those who didn't understand. God's Word is the only thing the devil seeks to take away from you, because every other thing in life stems from the Word. The devil comes around immediately the Word comes to you, and the purpose of his coming is to steal the Word from your heart.

When you hear the Word of the Kingdom and neglect to understand it, you're giving room to the devil to steal it from your heart. This is why you ought to have the Spirit of understanding at work in your life. He's the One Who helps you understand the Word of God that comes to you.

Understanding Comes By Revelation

"For this cause I Paul, the prisoner of Jesus Christ for you Gentiles, If ye have heard of the dispensation of the grace of God which is given me to youward: How that by revelation he made known unto me the mystery; (as I wrote afore in few

> **words, Whereby, when ye read, ye may understand my knowledge in the mystery of Christ)"**
>
> **(Ephesians 3:1-4).**

Paul explains here that God made the mystery of Christ known to him by revelation. The word "known" is translated from the Greek word "gnorizo," which means "to give to understand." In essence, Paul was saying that God, by revelation, gave him understanding of the mystery of Christ.

This presupposes that you cannot receive the understanding of a (spiritual) mystery by intellectual knowledge—not from school or anywhere else in the world. It comes by the revelation of the Holy Spirit.

Now, don't let anybody lie to you that you're not supposed to understand God's Word because the ordained minister is the only one gifted for that. That was what they said in the dark ages. They said only the pope and the priests could understand the Scriptures, and they kept God's people in darkness for hundreds of years.

The teacher may be anointed to teach the Word, but he's not more anointed to understand it than you are. So let no one keep you in bondage; it's been given to you to understand the mysteries of the Kingdom. That's what Jesus said!

Understanding Has Been Given To You!

Jesus always had a multitude gathered to listen to Him, but not all of the multitude were His disciples. So He would often speak to the multitude in parables. On one occasion, He had just told them the parable of the sower and none of them understood it, including the twelve apostles.

When He was away from the crowd, His disciples came to Him and asked, "Why speakest thou unto them in parables?" (Matthew 13:10).

Jesus then told them why He spoke in parables: *"Because it is given unto you to know the mysteries of the kingdom of heaven, but to them it is not given"* (Matthew 13:11).

This is marvellous. Even though the disciples didn't understand the parable at the time, Jesus said it was given to them to understand. The ability to understand it was theirs, they just didn't know it.

If you're a child of God, you have understanding of the mysteries of the Kingdom of Heaven. Jesus said so and you ought to be glad about it!

You say, "Well, I've been reading the Bible and I couldn't understand anything" or "I went to Church and listened to the message, but I really didn't understand what the preacher was saying." Stop talking that way! Talk in agreement with Jesus. He said it is given to you to know the mysteries of the Kingdom of Heaven; that's your inheritance.

That you didn't understand something doesn't mean it wasn't given to you to understand. There are times you don't understand certain things the first time you hear them, but you've been given the ability to understand them all the same. If you didn't seem to "catch" it the first time, what you should do is study some more. Get the tapes and books; listen to the tapes and read the books again and again, and through the power of the Spirit of understanding, you'll get to understand the truths.

So don't say you don't understand the Word that comes to you; it's been given to you to understand the things of the Kingdom.

Hear It, See It, Understand It And You'll Be 'Converted'

"For this people's heart is waxed gross, and their ears are dull of hearing, and their eyes they have closed; lest at any time they should see with their eyes, and hear with their ears, and should understand with their heart, and should be converted, and I should heal them"

(Matthew 13:15).

These are the words of Jesus, and if anybody knew the truth, Jesus did, for He is Himself Truth.

Here, Jesus lets us into a simple, but profound principle of God's Word: **If you ever see, hear, and understand the Word of God, you'll be converted.**

To be "converted" in this context means to have your situation turned around for good. In other words, you'll not have to put in any other effort to effect a change. Just hear the Word, see it, understand it, and it will automatically turn your situation around and change things in your life.

If you're in the Kingdom of God and have been born of His Spirit, then you've already been given an understanding heart. You're not trying to get it, nor are you praying for it. It's your present-hour possession. It belongs to you now!

The Spirit of understanding is at work in you. All you have to do now is recognize His presence in your life and He will reveal to you the mysteries of the Kingdom of God. Then you can have things change in your life and turn situations around in your favour.

5

THE SPIRIT OF COUNSEL

"And the spirit of the Lord shall rest upon him, the spirit of wisdom and understanding, the spirit of counsel..." (Isaiah 11:2).

The Spirit of counsel is the fourth of the seven Spirits of God listed in Isaiah 11:2. He is the One Who guides you. The psalmist, speaking of counsel, says,

"I will bless the LORD, who hath given me counsel: my reins also instruct me in the night seasons" (Psalm 16:7).

David talks about his "reins," that is, his inward man, instructing him in the night seasons. The Spirit of counsel instructs you and guides you from within. That's the Spirit by which the Lord guides your life.

Let's see something else about counsel in **Acts 16:6:**

> **"Now when they (Paul, Silas, and Timothy) had gone throughout Phrygia and the region of Galatia, and were forbidden of the Holy Ghost to preach the word in Asia."**

Notice it says they were forbidden of the Holy Ghost. Paul and his company wanted to go preach in Asia, but the Holy Ghost forbade them. Then again in Acts 16:7-9, we read that

> **"After they were come to Mysia, they assayed to go into Bithynia: but the Spirit suffered them not. And they passing by Mysia came down to Troas."**

This Spirit that dissuaded them from going into Bithynia was the Spirit of counsel. Also, in Acts 11, Peter recounted how the Spirit of counsel ministered to him while he was praying in the house of Simon the tanner:

> **"And, behold, immediately there were three men already come unto the house where I was, sent from Caesarea unto me. And the Spirit bade me go with them..."**
>
> **(Acts 11:11-12).**

The Spirit of counsel instructed Peter to go with these men and preach the gospel to them in Caesarea.

Remember the words of David in Psalm 16:7: "I will bless the Lord who has given me counsel. My reins (inward guide) also instruct me in the night seasons." That's the Spirit of counsel. He instructs you and tells you what to do and what not to do. He directs you in all your affairs.

You may have been headed in the wrong direction, but when the Spirit of counsel ministers to you, "you will hear a voice behind you say, "No, this is the way; walk here" (Isaiah 30:21 TLB).

The Spirit of Counsel is The Extraordinary Strategist

"...and his name shall be called Wonderful, Counsellor, The mighty God, The everlasting Father, The Prince of Peace"

(Isaiah 9:6).

The original Hebrew rendering of this portion of the Bible doesn't say, "Wonderful, Counsellor," two different names, as indicated here in the King James Version. It actually reads as one compound name: "Wonderful Counsellor." You'll observe that the other names, "Mighty God," "Everlasting Father," and "Prince of peace" with which the prophet describes the Lord, are also dualized.

The name "Wonderful Counsellor" means "Extraordinary Strategist." The Spirit of counsel is the Extraordinary Strategist. That means He's beyond the ordinary mind or senses. He's supernatural. He cannot be confused. He knows the way out of every crisis you face. He knows how you can come out of the darkness; He knows how to make you a success. He's your Extraordinary Strategist and He lives inside you.

Let's look at one of His extraordinary strategies: Moses had just led the children of Israel out of captivity in Egypt. But Pharaoh wasn't about to let them go that easily, and he sent his entire army in hot pursuit of the "defenceless" Israelites. They were in a fix. Before them spread out the wide expanse of the Red Sea. Right behind them, they could hear the thundering hoofs of horses and ominous clatter of chariots as the Egyptian army bore down on them.

Humanly speaking, there was no way of escape. But as far as the Extraordinary Strategist was concerned, there was nothing like "no way out." That's why I tell people: "The walls in front of you don't exist; the barriers are not real. Close your eyes; keep walking in the Name of Jesus, and they'll get out of your way!"

When the people cried out to Moses, he in turn cried out to God, but God's response was simply amazing. He said, "*...Why do you cry to Me? Tell the children of Israel to go forward. "But lift up your rod, and stretch out your hand over the sea and divide it. And the children of Israel shall go on dry ground through the midst of the sea*" (Exodus 14:15-16 NKJV).

The Extraordinary Strategist told Moses to stretch his rod over the water and divide it. Moses did as he was told and the children of Israel were miraculously delivered. The Red Sea parted and they went through on dry ground, but the entire Egyptian army was destroyed in the same sea.

Now if you were Moses or the children of Israel, you wouldn't want to go forward if just anybody told you to do that, but because it was coming from the Extraordinary Strategist, it worked.

Jehoshaphat's Extraordinary Strategist in the Face of War

There's another instance of the Extraordinary Strategist's superb counselling prowess in **2 Chronicles 20:1,3-4:**

> **"It came to pass after this also, that the children of Moab, and the children of Ammon, and with them other beside the Ammonites, came against Jehoshaphat to battle... And Jehoshaphat feared, and set himself to seek the Lord, and proclaimed a fast throughout all Judah. And Judah gathered themselves together, to ask help of the Lord: even out of all the cities of Judah they came to seek the Lord"**

The small nation of Judah was completely surrounded and outnumbered by the armies of three enemy nations–Moab, Ammon, and Mount Seir. So King Jehoshaphat proclaimed a fast throughout the land, and the entire nation, as one, sought the face of the Lord.

While they prayed and fasted, there was a word of prophecy. The Spirit of the Lord (the Extraordinary Strategist) came upon Jahaziel, a Levite, and He gave the king and the people the strategy they required to win the battle. He told them: "You don't have to fight in this battle, for the battle is not yours but the Lord's. Tomorrow, you go out against the enemy; they're camping by the cliff of Ziz. Put twenty singers ahead of your army. They're not to carry any weapons of war but just sing into the war front" (2 Chronicles 20:15-17).

And that's exactly what Judah did. They marched to the camp of the enemy with twenty singers ahead of them, singing, "Praise the Lord, for His mercy endureth forever!"

As they sang, the angels of God were activated; they entered the enemy's camp and began to slay them. Pandemonium broke out and the enemy soldiers, not knowing what hit them, turned their swords on one another and started killing one another. By the time God's people got into their enemies' camp, they were all dead! (2 Chronicles 20:22-24).

No wonder Paul said, *"the weapons of our warfare are not carnal, but mighty through God to the pulling down of strong holds;) Casting down imaginations, and every high thing that exalteth itself against the knowledge of God, and bringing into captivity every thought to the obedience of Christ;"* (2 Corinthians 10:4-5). Hallelujah!

It doesn't matter what you're going through or how hopeless the situation looks, you can still shout, "Praise the Lord!" because your Extraordinary Strategist will show you what to do and you'll come out victoriously!

He's Your Miracle-Producing Counsellor

The term "Wonderful Counsellor" in Isaiah 9:6 also refers to the counsel of a king. In Micah 4:9, the prophet asks, *"Now why dost thou cry out aloud? is there no king in thee? is thy counsellor perished? for pangs have taken thee as a woman in travail,"* thus equating the king with the counsellor. He's dealing here with the wise counsel of a king, counsel backed up with power.

The Hebrew word translated "wonderful" here actually means "mighty acts and deeds, miraculous works." So he's talking about miracle-producing counsel that comes from a king, and that can only be the Lord, Who gives you counsel within that produces miracles without.

I'll give you a simple example: Only the Lord could have told Moses, "Take your shepherd's rod, go to Pharaoh and wield that rod before him and there would be miracles." Only the counsel of the Lord could have instructed him, "Hold that rod in your hand, stand before the rock, strike it, and water will come out."

Ordinarily, this counsel doesn't seem to make any sense, but the Bible says where the word of a king is there is power (Ecclesiastes 8:4), and we're talking about the counsel of not just any king, but the King of kings!

ISAAC'S COUNSELLOR IN A TIME OF FAMINE

At a certain time, there was a prolonged dry season all over the land of Canaan. Famine had set in and many people were leaving for Egypt. Then God told Isaac, *"Sojourn in this land, and I will be with thee, and will bless thee; for unto thee, and unto thy seed, I will give all these countries, and I will perform the oath which I sware unto Abraham thy father; And I will make thy seed to multiply as the stars of heaven, and will give unto thy seed all these countries; and in thy seed shall all the nations of the earth be blessed;"* (Genesis 26:3-4).

True to His words, every time Isaac went somewhere and dug the ground, he struck water, and the people couldn't understand it. Nobody else found water; even though they dug deep, they still couldn't get water. But when Isaac came and dug right beside them, water came out!

During this period, everyone lost his crop as

the famine was severe. But Isaac had counsel from within. He had been told by the Lord, *"Stay in this land...and I will be with you and bless you"* (Genesis 26:2-3a TEV). So in the midst of severe famine and drought, *"Isaac sowed in that land, and received in the same year an hundredfold: and the Lord blessed him. And the man waxed great, and went forward, and grew until he became very great:* (Genesis 26:12-13). Isaac had a miracle-producing Counsellor!

Counsel such as those illustrated in this chapter all had to have come from the mouth of God; otherwise, they would have failed woefully and resulted in utter disaster! However, this is the Spirit of counsel at work. Isaiah calls Him your Wonderful Counsellor. He is your miracle-producing Counsellor, your Extraordinary Strategist. When He tells you to do something, it may sound illogical, but it's miracle-producing counsel. That's what makes it wonderful; that's why it's a miracle when such counsel brings forth outstanding results.

Do you have the Spirit of counsel? Has He ever instructed you? Are you acquainted with Him or do you find yourself always getting advice from people? Let the Extraordinary Strategist function in you, and He'll instruct you on the right steps to take in your every endeavour. Take advantage of Him today. Receive His counsel and you will have direction.

6

THE SPIRIT OF MIGHT

Isaiah 11:1-2: "And there shall come forth a rod out of the stem of Jesse, and a Branch shall grow out of his roots: And the spirit of the Lord shall rest upon him, the spirit of wisdom and understanding, THE SPIRIT OF counsel and MIGHT..."

The Spirit of might is the fifth of the seven Spirits of God listed in Isaiah 11:2. There was one man in the Old Testament who operated frequently in the Spirit of might. He was a judge in Israel and Samson was his name.

Samson didn't have the Spirit of wisdom as Moses or Joshua had, otherwise, he wouldn't have done some of the dumb things he did. But he had the Spirit of might.

Judges 14:5-6:
"Then went Samson down, and his father and his mother, to Timnath, and came to the vineyards of Timnath: and, behold, a young lion roared against him. And the Spirit of the Lord came mightily upon him, and he rent him as he would have rent a kid, and he had nothing in his hand: but he told not his father or his mother what he had done."

A young lion roared at Samson and attacked him as he made his way through the vineyards of Timnath. To appreciate the great peril Samson was in, you must understand what a young lion is. It's not a cub or a weak, old lion that's ready to die, but a young, strong lion in its prime.

When Samson saw the lion, he didn't cry out,

"Daddy, help!" He didn't wonder, "Which way do I run?!" because in that instant, the Spirit of the Lord came mightily upon him and he got hold of the lion and tore it apart as he would have a little lamb. And he did it with his bare hands! When he was done, he didn't go around town telling everybody, "Guess what I just did!" He went on his way as though he'd just swatted a fly.

There's more about this man that I want you to see:

> **"And when he came unto Lehi, the Philistines shouted against him: and the Spirit of the Lord came mightily upon him, and the cords that were upon his arms became as flax that was burnt with fire, and his bands loosed from off his hands. And he found a new jawbone of an ass, and put forth his hand, and took it, and *slew a thousand men therewith*"**
>
> **(Judges 15:14-15).**

The men of Judah had bound Samson and delivered him to the Philistines at Lehi. When the Philistines saw him bound and came charging toward him, the Spirit of the Lord came mightily upon him again and he snapped his bands loose as if they were flax in the fire. Then he took a jawbone of an ass and killed a thousand of them with it.

These were not just one thousand ordinary men; they were armed men of war that had been trained in combat. It wasn't because Samson was a strong man that he was able to destroy them; the Bible tells us how he did it—the Spirit of the Lord came ***mightily*** upon him.

When the Spirit of might came upon Samson, he was a changed man. This doesn't mean he didn't know himself or what he was doing anymore. But when that Spirit came on him, He took over his senses and his body, so he couldn't think or act like an ordinary man. That was why he could do extraordinary things.

I know that David must have read about Samson and was inspired by his testimonies. Then the day came when Samuel, the prophet of God, came to his father's house and poured oil on his head. After he had done that, he told David, "Now you're anointed by the Holy Spirit," and from then on the Spirit of the Lord rested upon David. He went back to taking care of his father's sheep, but he was a different man; he was carrying the anointing.

One of those days, a lion came to take a lamb from his flock. Other men would have fled, but David, being full of the Spirit, charged after the lion, delivered the lamb from its mouth, and killed it. He said, "I caught it by its beard." That's marvellous!

Another time, a bear came to take one of the lambs as David tended the flock and it met the same fate as the lion. Also, when he faced Goliath of Gath, the Philistine giant, he told him he would end up like those beasts he had killed, and that was exactly what happened.

These feats of magnificent gallantry were not done in David's own strength but by the anointing of the Spirit of might that was upon him.

Might That Overcomes Strength

When the Spirit of might is at work in you, He'll cause you to be bold, and I'm not just talking about you trying to muster boldness or trying to remember Scriptures to quote when trouble strikes. The Spirit of might, not only gives you boldness, but also brings you might that overcomes strength.

Isaiah prophesied concerning the Lord Jesus in Isaiah 9:6 and called Him "The Mighty God." This is one of those beautiful names of God and it's not referring to might in terms of size, but that attribute of might that overcomes. It's talking about a demonstration of strength in such a way that it overpowers the strong.

"Might" is one of those words the English language really doesn't have a perfect definition for, but it's an overpowering force. It's that which overcomes and surpasses strength itself. It refers to extraordinary power.

Samson had the Spirit of might. He got to the city gate of Gaza one day and pulled it out, poles, bars and all! You can imagine how heavy a city gate should be. Well, Samson not only pulled this one out, he put it on his shoulder and carried it far away from town to the top of a hill! That's might!

But Samson did even more. After the Philistines had captured him and gouged his eyes, they brought him out to entertain them during a great feast they were having in the temple of Dagon. Then Samson prayed, *"O Lord God, remember me, I pray thee, and strengthen me, I pray thee, only this once, O God, that I may be at once avenged of the Philistines for my two eyes"* (Judges 16:28). After he had prayed thus, the Spirit of might came upon him and gave him superhuman strength as before.

Suddenly, his muscles began to bulge. When he placed his hands on the two middle pillars of the temple and started heaving against them, his captors thought he was kidding and started laughing at him.

However, some were uneasy and they said, "Did you hear that cracking noise? I thought I heard something breaking."

Others reassured them, "Stop worrying; he's just entertaining us," and they continued drinking, eating and laughing at Samson as he busied himself with the pillars.

Then the cracking noise increased and dust started falling from parts of the column as it cracked. A hush immediately fell on the temple and someone whispered, "Hey, don't you think we should stop him now?"

Someone else in the crowd shouted, "Oh, come on! Can't you see the size of those pillars? It's impossible for him to bring them down. More wine!" and everybody laughed and promptly resumed their revelling. But before they knew what was happening, huge slabs of rock started pelting down as the supporting columns gave way. Their laughter turned into screams of terror as they were crushed under the huge stones that fell from everywhere in the building.

Samson brought the whole building down on over three thousand people and not one of them escaped; he killed more Philistines in his death than in his lifetime. He was indeed a mighty man of valour, the champion of Israel.

Now I know you're thinking, "Well, that was Samson; no normal human being could do that!" You're right. But if you're born again, you're not a "normal" human being. You've been called into a life of the supernatural and you ought to have the Spirit of might functioning in you to live that life, for He's the One Who empowers you to do superhuman things.

Be Strengthened With Might

Paul prayed a beautiful prayer for the Ephesian Church but it is also a prayer of the Spirit for all God's children:

"For this cause I bow my knees unto the

Father of our Lord Jesus Christ, of whom the whole family in Heaven and earth is named that He would grant you according to the riches of His glory to be strengthened with might by His Spirit in the inner man"

(Ephesians 3:14-16).

"Might" is from the Greek word "dunamis." Remember that in Acts 1:8, Jesus said to His disciples, *"Ye shall receive* ***power*** *after that the Holy Ghost is come upon you." The word "power"* in Acts 1:8 is from the same Greek word "dunamis" translated "might" in Ephesians 3:16.

Power is the inherent, dynamic ability to cause changes. If you want changes in your body, family, job, or finances, you received the inherent, dynamic ability to effect those changes when you received the Holy Ghost!

However, when Paul prayed for the Church to be strengthened or invigorated from within, he used the word *"might"* instead of *"power."* There's a reason for his choosing the word *"might"* this time. You must understand that the scriptures were given to us with words carefully chosen by the Holy Ghost, and He guided Paul to use the word "might" in order to communicate His mind to us.

"Might" in Ephesians 3:16 connotes miracle-working power. So Paul's prayer is that we be invigorated with miracle-working power, not in the church, but in our spirits.

This mighty power overcomes strength, and God wants it working in us. Therefore, I give you the same charge Paul gave the Ephesian church: *"Finally, my brethren, be strong in the Lord, and in the power of his might"* (Ephesians 6:10). Become conscious of the presence of the Spirit of might and allow Him to have expression in and through you.

7

THE SPIRIT OF KNOWLEDGE

Most times, the difference between a successful, victorious Christian and the one who's not is not so much their gifts, but the knowledge they have.

Your limitations and your achievements today are a direct function and clear reflection of your knowledge or the lack of it. But with the right kind of knowledge, you can always be greater and better than you presently are.

The focus in this chapter is on the Spirit of knowledge, but first we must understand what real knowledge is, for until we do, we cannot appreciate or recognize the ministry of the Spirit of knowledge in our lives.

Revelation Knowledge

Knowledge, according to the Webster Dictionary, is "the fact or condition of being aware of something, or knowing something with familiarity gained through experience or association." It also means "acquaintance with or understanding of a science, art, or technique." Knowledge could also mean "the circumstance or condition of apprehending truth or fact through reasoning."

However, these definitions would not suffice for the kind of knowledge we're dealing with here–knowledge that comes by the Spirit–**revelation knowledge.**

Revelation knowledge is exact knowledge. It is specific, specialized and absolute knowledge. It is far removed from sense knowledge, which the Webster Dictionary has so articulately defined for us. Revelation knowledge is knowledge from the

Spirit of God that is imparted to your human spirit without any material medium. It is not a knowledge of the senses; it therefore transcends the mental realm. In the arena of revelation knowledge, there are no assumptions. You just know that you know what you know.

Heart-Knowledge Versus Head-Knowledge

There's an astronomical difference between sense-knowledge and revelation knowledge, and the incognizance of that difference has caused many Christians frustrations in their lives. They feel they know God's Word better than the results they're experiencing in their lives indicate. So they keep wondering and asking, "What's the problem? Why am I not getting better results than these?"

The problem with such people is that the knowledge is in their heads and not their hearts. That's the reason they just can't seem to put what they know to work and get better results.

You can't really say you've known anything

that is of God or from God if you haven't received it as a revelation in your spirit. Revelation knowledge is of the Spirit, and it's a light through which God guides your spirit. Sense knowledge, however, is a gamble.

When you *know* something by revelation, you'd walk in the light of it. The fact that you walk in it is evidence of your knowledge.

I've had people ask me, "What if you know something but don't put it to use?"

If it's revelation knowledge, that'll be very difficult. It will be the most difficult thing to know God's Word in your spirit and not live or act accordingly. When someone says he knows what to do but doesn't do it, what he has is mere sense knowledge. That knowledge is in his head and not his heart. He may even talk it, but it won't work, because it's mere information in his brain and not a life-force proceeding from his heart.

However, revelation knowledge works differently; it spurs you to action. When you *really know* something in your spirit, you'll do it. If you don't do it, that's proof-positive you don't know it.

It's practically impossible to not act on what you know in your spirit. That's because as the revelation knowledge of God's Word comes into your spirit, something happens within you. It works in your mind, renews your thinking, and becomes in you a vital force that causes you to live accordingly. It produces what it talks about in you and moves you from one level of glory to another. Revelation knowledge imparts wisdom to you, praise God!

The Spirit of Knowledge Brings Awareness

> **"Now we have received, not the spirit of the world, but the spirit which is of God; that we might know the things that are freely given to us of God"**
>
> **(1 Corinthians 2:12).**

What Paul is saying here is quite instructive and we can get the import of it from the Greek text. For the word translated "know" here, Paul used a Greek word "eido," which means "to become aware." Replacing "know" with the phrase "become aware of" gives us a better picture of what he's showing us:

> **"...we have received, not the spirit of the world, but the spirit which is of God; that we might become aware of the things that are freely given to us of God."**
>
> **(1 Corinthians 2:12).**

This is a very significant point, but what does it mean? Think about it this way: You're brought into a large, dark building you've never been in before. Then someone turns on the lights, and suddenly, you become aware there are things in there–furniture, home entertainment systems, electronic gadgets, computers, lights, switches, doors, locks, e.t.c. You *become aware* that all these things are there in the house.

This is the first thing that happens when the

Spirit of knowledge comes into your life. He turns on the light in your life and you become aware of the things that are yours in Christ.

However, the fact that you're now aware of all the things in the house and that they're there for you to use doesn't mean you know how they function or how to operate them. So, even though you're in the house and you're aware that all the things in it are yours to use, you may still be at a loss.

This is why many uninformed believers find themselves feeling lost. They've come into this new kind of life, but nothing seems to be working. So they wonder, "Are these things for real or have I made a mistake?" No you haven't made a mistake. The Spirit of knowledge has only just made you aware. But there's more He wants to do than just bring you an awareness.

The Spirit of Knowledge Brings You Full Understanding

Ephesians 3:17-19,
"That Christ may dwell in your hearts by faith; that ye, being rooted and grounded in love, May be able to comprehend with all saints what is the breadth, and length, and depth, and height; And to know the love of Christ, which passeth knowledge, that ye might be filled with all the fulness of God."

Observe Paul's choice of words carefully; he said, *"And to **know** the love of Christ which surpasses **knowledge**."* How can you know something that surpasses knowledge? What was he talking about when he said for us to have the knowledge of the love of Christ that surpasses knowledge?

There are two words here I want you to mark: *"Know"* and *"Knowledge."*

The Greek word translated "know" is "Ginosko." It refers to revelation knowledge, which is absolute knowledge. So Paul was saying in essence, *"And to **have the absolute knowledge of** the love of Christ,"* which means, "to know the love of Christ by revelation."

For the other word, *"knowledge,"* Paul chooses the Greek word "gnosis," which is knowledge based on science, a discovery.

Putting both together, Paul would have said, "to ***'ginosko'*** the love of Christ which surpasses ***'gnosis'***" that is, "to ***have a revelation*** of the love of Christ which surpasses ***scientific knowledge or human discovery***." He was talking about knowing the love of Christ beyond your senses and human definitions, but according to revelation. And this doesn't just happen; it comes by the Spirit of knowledge.

He "Brings You Into" Esoteric Knowledge

This is yet another ministry of the Spirit of knowledge: He brings you into esoteric knowledge:

> **"That the communication [participation] of thy faith may become effectual by the acknowledging of every good thing which is in you in Christ Jesus"**
>
> **(Philemon 1:6).**

Here, Paul chooses another word, "epignosis," which is translated *"acknowledging."* You may have observed that there are similarities between all these Greek words, but there are also very significant nuances of meaning that must be clearly understood.

"Epignosis" is a derivative of another Greek word "epiginosko" (which is actually a combination of two root words, "epi" and "ginosko"), and it means to recognize, perceive, or *become fully acquainted with.* It doesn't just imply an awareness, but a bringing into esoteric knowledge, a discernment, a full understanding of the subject.

I call it a "bringing into esoteric knowledge," because, not only does this knowledge come to you, you're brought into it. And it's esoteric because it's knowledge meant only for the "initiated." This is what the Spirit of Knowledge does–He brings you into esoteric knowledge.

Paul says the communication of your faith becomes effective by the "*epignosis*" of every good thing in you in Christ Jesus. This means that as you're brought into this full and special knowledge of all the good things that are in you in Christ Jesus, the sharing of your faith becomes more productive.

Do you know the good things which are in you in Christ Jesus? You can only know them and understand them fully through the Spirit of knowledge. Not only will He help you discover, He'll also bring you into the full knowledge of these things and how to put them to work. Then you would have a super life, praise God!

You Have "Ginosko"

"Howbeit we speak wisdom among them that are perfect: yet not the wisdom of this world, nor of the princes of this world, that come to nought: But we speak the wisdom of God in a mystery (esoteric language), even the hidden wisdom, which God ordained before the world unto our glory: Which none of the princes of this world knew: for had they known (ginosko) it, they would not have crucified the Lord of glory"

(1 Corinthians 2:6-8).

The rulers of the world in Jesus' day had no *ginosko*—revelation knowledge—for had they had *ginosko,* they would not have crucified the Lord of glory. But thank God, it's different with us:

"But as it is written, Eye hath not seen, nor ear heard, neither have entered into the heart of man, the things which God hath prepared for them that love him. But

God hath revealed them unto us by his Spirit: for the Spirit searcheth all things, yea, the deep things of God"

(1 Corinthians 2:9-10).

This is the Spirit of Knowledge at work in us. By Him, God reveals all these things to us. We're not at a loss. We're not trying to find out about God. There's a revelation of God granted us by His Spirit.

Remember, the first thing He does is to make you aware of all the things that are yours in Christ, then He brings you into full knowledge of them. However, the question now is: What does this knowledge mean to you and what can you do with it? How does it affect you?

When you come into full knowledge and understanding of these things, your mentality is affected. There are certain ways you just can't reason anymore. Your mind (your whole mentality and thinking processes) becomes renewed through the Word.

Many people remain in a sorry state even after they've been born again because they refuse revelation knowledge. God Himself said, *"My people are destroyed* (crushed, brought under, made poor, oppressed) *for lack of knowledge"* (Hosea 4:6). This is not the lack of knowledge of economics, government, physics or theology; He's talking about lack of "ginosko," which is revelation knowledge or spiritual knowledge of God's Word.

When revelation knowledge comes into your spirit, it enlightens you and catapults you to a higher realm of life. And when you start living according to revelation knowledge, people would think you're a boaster, because you don't think or talk like the rest of the world.

Get acquainted with the Spirit of knowledge. He is the Teacher; He will teach you the Word of God and impart to your spirit the revelations of God's Word that will cause you to walk in His wisdom, power, and glory. Hallelujah!

8

THE SPIRIT OF THE FEAR OF THE LORD

"And the spirit of the Lord shall rest upon him, the spirit of wisdom and understanding, the spirit of counsel and might, the spirit of knowledge and of the fear of the Lord;"

(Isaiah 11:2).

Now we meet the last, but not the least, of the seven Spirits of God listed in Isaiah 11:2. The Spirit of the fear of the Lord is also referred to as the **Spirit of reverence. Psalm 111:4-10** tells us:

"He hath made his wonderful works to be remembered: the Lord is gracious and full of compassion. He hath given meat unto them that fear him: he will ever be mindful of his covenant. He hath shewed his people the power of his works, that he may give them the heritage of the heathen. The works of his hands are verity and judgment; all his commandments are sure. They stand fast for ever and ever, and are done in truth and uprightness. He sent redemption unto his people: he hath commanded his covenant for ever: *holy and reverend* is his name. The fear of the Lord is the beginning of wisdom: a good understanding have all they that do his commandments: his praise endureth for ever."

This is the Spirit that worked with the priests in the Old Testament. Samuel was both prophet and priest to the children of Israel, and the Bible says he *"called to the LORD, and the LORD sent thunder and rain that day; and all the people greatly feared the* L*ORD and Samuel"* (1 Samuel 12:18). That was orchestrated by the Spirit of the fear of the Lord.

THE SPIRIT OF THE FEAR OF THE LORD INSISTS ON REVERENCE

When this Spirit of reverence comes into a place, things change. He disciplines people and sets things in order. He does something big and everybody becomes quiet and humble in God's presence. You've got to watch out for this Spirit! When Ananias and Sapphira misbehaved, He struck them dead and great fear came upon the people (Acts 5:1-11).

Any time the anointing of God's Spirit is so strong and something spectacular like this happens, fear (holy awe, reverence) comes upon the people. That's the Spirit of the fear of the Lord in action. He insists that you have reverence for God and for the things of God.

Some people come late for a church service and just walk around as if they own the whole place. They go from row to row, looking for a good seat while the message is going on, and distracting everybody in the process. Such people have no reverence!

If you're like that, you've got to be careful. Next time you're late for a service and the message is on, find a seat quickly, because there's a Spirit in that place Who doesn't take kindly to an irreverent attitude.

Sometimes, in a meeting, a word of the Spirit is given and a call is made. At such times, there has to be reverence. For instance, the minister may say, "There's a man here who's being healed of arthritis. I want that man to come forward." If a woman decides to come forward even when she heard clearly that the call was for a man, such a woman doesn't have that Spirit of the fear of the Lord in her. I've seen people like that knocked down under the anointing of God's Spirit!

Understand what I'm talking about. There's a time when the Spirit of God comes into a place and He insists on absolute reverence.

They didn't have such reverence in the early Corinthian church. Even though they were walking in the manifestations of the gifts of the Spirit, they lacked the Spirit of the fear of the Lord. They were scrambling for food meant for the Holy Communion (1 Corinthians 11:20-22). They were committing abominable sins (1 Corinthians 5:1) and there was so much envy, strife and division among them (1 Corinthians 3:3-4). They had no reverence for spiritual things.

Submit And Be Humble

There's something about the Spirit of the fear of the Lord that produces humility in you. He instils in you the fear (reverence) of God and makes you say the right words.

Insulting words cannot come out of your mouth when you have the Spirit of the fear of the Lord. He makes you humble. It doesn't matter who's chairing a meeting in which you're present, you remain humble because you recognize He's in that place.

The apostle Paul said, *"Submitting yourselves one to another in the fear of God."* Take Peter's advice in 1 Peter 5:5-6: *"all of you be subject one to another, and be clothed with humility: for God resisteth the proud, and giveth grace to the humble. Humble yourselves therefore under the mighty hand of God, that he may exalt you in due time:"*

Yield yourself to this Spirit. He will cause you to walk in reverence and humility, and exalt you in the due course of time.

9

THE FULLNESS OF THE SPIRIT

Now you understand that the Holy Spirit can function in your life in a greater measure and you can participate fully in the divine nature.

When all seven Spirits of God are functioning in your life, there'll be no confusion. You'll be balanced. You'll be full of power by the Spirit of the Lord and the Spirit of might.

You'll also be full of the Word because of the Spirit of wisdom, the Spirit of knowledge, the Spirit of understanding, and the Spirit of counsel.

And then, the Spirit of the fear of the Lord will balance these up with humility. You will not become puffed up because of the abundance of power and revelation manifested in your life.

In **Ephesians 3:16-19**, Paul prays for the Ephesian Christians:

> **That he (God) would grant you, according to the riches of his glory, to be strengthened with might by his Spirit in the inner man; That Christ may dwell in your hearts by faith; that ye, being rooted and grounded in love, May be able to comprehend with all saints what is the breadth, and length, and depth, and height; And to know the love of Christ, which passeth knowledge, that ye might be filled with all the fulness of God."**

This is so beautiful. Here we see Paul praying for the manifestation of the Spirit of might, the Spirit of understanding, and the Spirit of knowledge. Then he caps it all up when he prays, "that ye might be filled with all the fullness of God." That's depicting all the seven Spirits of God. If this was good and necessary for the Ephesian Christians, we need it even more today.

God really wants to do something in your life. It's not right for you to walk only in a measure of God's Spirit; you'll lose out that way. You need to be filled with all the fullness of God's Spirit.

Make Room For The Spirit

Now the question is: Do you have room in your life for the Spirit? Is there still any space in your heart for Him or have you clogged your heart with all kinds of cares and concerns? You must consciously get rid of the dross and make room for the Spirit in your life.

In **Luke 4:18,** Jesus said,

> **"The Spirit of the Lord is upon me, because he hath anointed me to preach the gospel to the poor; he hath sent me to heal the brokenhearted, to preach deliverance to the captives, and recovering of sight to the blind, to set at liberty them that are bruised,"**

The Spirit of the Lord is the One Who helps you with power to do things, and He's functioning in you even now as you read. You may be a minister reading this book; you've got to have the Spirit of the Lord anoint you. That unction has to be there in your ministry, otherwise, it will be empty.

Remember, the Holy Spirit of God is a Person. He's not a thing, nor is He fluid, oil, water, a cloud or gas. So don't think, "Well, they poured the anointing oil on me to ordain me. If it was on me then, it's still on me now."

True, the anointing came on you the day you were ordained a minister, but how much anointing are you walking in now? For some people, all they've got left in their life is only one of the seven Spirits of God, Who's there just to make sure they get to heaven. It ought not to be that way. You can be filled with all the fullness of God!

Remember, the Bible says, these seven Spirits of God have been sent forth into all the earth (Revelation 5:6). This means the Spirit of God in

His full manifestation is working all over the world. He's always doing something big with those who walk with Him.

There may be a Christian whose life is empty and uninspiring. All he does is read one or two verses everyday and pray some religious prayer: "O God, thank You for yesterday, today and tomorrow. Bless me and my family. Bless everybody. Bless the whole world. Plus God, minus devil, in Jesus' Name. Amen." That's about all he knows to pray!

For some others, they pray today to cover the entire week. They say they don't have time to pray in the mornings because they go to work very early. So they pray all their prayer for the week at every Sunday service. They say, "Lord, this is for Monday, Tuesday, Wednesday, Thursday, Friday, and Saturday," and they pray extra hard, imagining that they're stocking their prayer reservoir full for the week. So they go on to do whatever they like from Monday to Saturday. Come another Sunday, they're in church, ready for another weekly stockpiling of prayer. God doesn't want you living like that.

When God sent manna from heaven to feed the children of Israel, He told them, "You've got to eat today's manna today. Don't keep some for tomorrow, for tomorrow, there'll be a fresh one for you to eat" (Exodus 16:19).

This is letting us know we're supposed to receive the ministry of the Spirit everyday, because we require His guidance in our lives everyday. Yesterday's guidance will not suffice for today, and today's will not suffice for tomorrow. We have to have a relationship with Him today, and in the "now" of our lives. We must walk with the Spirit and in the Spirit today!

How To Pray And Be Filled With The Spirit

If you would pray and get filled with the Holy Spirit and let Him take charge of your day, you'll begin to experience tremendous increase in every area of your life. That's why you've got to learn to pray like this:

"Father, in the Name of the Lord Jesus, I understand from the Word of God that You'll take charge of my circumstances if I let You. You are the Lord of my life, and I pray that You order my steps today in the course that You've already planned for me. I want to meet only the people that You plan for me to meet today, and hear the things that You plan for me to hear, and say the things You plan for me to say.

"I function as a child of God today in the anointing of the Holy Ghost. I walk in Your light, in the Name of the Lord Jesus. There's nobody coming into my world as an accident today. The Spirit of dominion is at work in me today, in the Name of the Lord Jesus.

"I refuse to fear, for though I walk through the valley of the shadow of death, I fear no evil, for You are with me; Your rod and Your staff comfort me. I refuse to be defeated today, for I'm a victor in Christ Jesus. I'm more than a conqueror, in the Name of the Lord Jesus.

"Thank You Lord for Your presence is with me today. I thank You for the Spirit of excellence is at work in me. I do not act foolishly or utter a foolish word. The wisdom of God is found in my mouth, and I give counsel by the Spirit today. I deal with people by the Spirit today. I see with the eyes of God today, in the Name of the Lord Jesus Christ.

"Oh Lord God, I thank You, because good things are coming my way today. I receive in the Name of the Lord Jesus. And I'm a giver today; I'm a blesser today, in the Name of the Lord Jesus. My body is

yielded to You, every fibre of my being and every bone of my body is for the Holy Ghost. I'm Your living tabernacle today. Talk through me; move through me; walk in me; talk in me, in the Name of the Lord Jesus.

"The health of God is in me. I refuse to let my body be subject to sickness, disease and infirmity. Every fibre of my being is inundated by the life of God. I'm walking in divine health, in the Name of Jesus. Glory to God!"

How can you be defeated when you pray like this? Your spirit has arisen to the occasion! Don't quit praying at this point, because there's more. You continue and declare:

"Lord, I thank You for the Spirit of understanding and the Spirit of knowledge are functioning in me. I study the Word of God today and I understand it. I can see the Word, I can hear the Word, I can

understand the Word and so it's working in me, and my mouth cannot be shut. I will speak boldly concerning the things of God and the revelations of God that I receive, in the Name of the Lord Jesus.

"The nations of the world are waiting for me and I'm coming in the Name of the Lord. I've been commissioned and sent of God. I've got a message from Him to the world, and they will hear it, in the Name of Jesus. Watch out world, I'm coming!"

You can also pray in the Spirit for your family members and the people you work with. You can rephrase this prayer to suit you, and include the names of your family members, friends, colleagues, etc. in the appropriate places:

"I thank You Father for my children. The anointing is upon them. They can't but do the will of God. They can't but work the works of God. They can't but live in

the Word of God, in the Name of Jesus. No devil hatched out of hell can touch them. I thank You Father, for Wisdom is in the mouth of my wife and in her heart. She functions in the things of God today, in the Name of the Lord Jesus.

"I pray for every one of my staff in the Name of Jesus. They cannot but do the will of God and think the thoughts of God. In their going out and in their coming in, not one of them is subject to the devil. The Word of God is in their hearts and in their mouths in the Name of the Lord Jesus!"

Glory to God! This is how I pray. Now, isn't this better than praying, "Oh God, help me. Oh God, bless me, Oh God deliver me..."?

I can't pray dumb and negative prayers. I lift my hands up to God and declare, *"Father, I'm so blessed. I'm such a blessed man. I don't know how to thank You enough, for You've blessed me so much, I'm embarrassed. You said in Your Word that You've blessed me and I looked at my life and found it so, and everybody that comes into my world is blessed. Glory to God, I'm blessed!"*

This is the way I pray, because this is the way He told us to pray. When I pray like this, I get full of the Holy Ghost. Sometimes I say, *"Lord, You told us to be filled with the Spirit, speaking to ourselves in psalms and hymns. Now, I'm going to make You some psalms and sing You some hymns..."* and when I start doing that, I get full of God's Spirit.

Even now as you're reading, God's Spirit is already working in you. Something is happening in your spirit right now. The fire of the Holy Ghost is burning in your heart. So don't wait; get in the flow!

Go ahead and begin to worship God and thank Him. Begin to declare His Word in prayer, praise, and prophecy. Speak to yourself in psalms, hymns, and spiritual songs, and you will be filled with the Spirit.

Remember, we've been made kings and priests unto God (Revelation 1:6). So begin to pray in the Holy Ghost. Sing in the Holy Ghost. Dance in the Spirit. Laugh in the Spirit. Keep praising God and rejoicing in His presence, for in His presence, there's fullness of joy. Don't hold back. Get so full of the Holy Ghost until you're drunk in Him. That's where you function in all seven Spirits of God, and that's the secret to a life of the unending miraculous.

To contact the author write:

Pastor Chris Oyakhilome:

United Kingdom:

Christ Embassy Int'l office

363 Springfield Road

Chelmsford, Essex, CM2 6AW

Tel:+44 1245 490 234

South Africa:

303 Pretoria Avenue

Cnr.Harley and Hendrik Verwoerd,

Randburg, Gauteng, South Africa.

Tel:+27-11-326 0971,

+27-11-326 0972

Nigeria:

Christ Embassy Church

P.O. Box 13563, Ikeja,

Lagos, Nigeria.

Tel:+234-8023324187-9

or email:pastorchris@christembassy.org

Please include your testimony or help received from this book when you write.

Your prayer requests are also welcome.

OTHER BOOKS BY
PASTOR CHRIS OYAKHILOME

- PROPHECY: UNDERSTANDING THE POWER THAT CONTROLS YOUR FUTURE
- HOW TO MAKE YOUR FAITH WORK
- PRAYING THE RIGHT WAY
- THE POWER OF TONGUES
- THE GATES OF ZION
- JOIN THIS CHARIOT
- DON'T STOP HERE!
- 7 THINGS THE HOLY SPIRIT WILL DO IN YOU
- 7 THINGS THE HOLY SPIRIT WILL DO FOR YOU
- WHEN GOD VISITS YOU
- HOW TO RECEIVE A MIRACLE AND RETAIN IT
- NOW THAT YOU ARE BORN AGAIN
- THE HOLY SPIRIT AND YOU
- NONE OF THESE DISEASES
- THE OIL AND THE MANTLE
- YOUR RIGHTS IN CHRIST
- KEEPING YOUR HEALING
- THE PROMISED LAND
- RECREATING YOUR WORLD
- RHAPSODY OF REALITIES DAILY DEVOTIONAL
- RHAPSODY OF REALITIES TOPICAL COMPENDIUM (VOL 1)

BOOKS BY
PASTOR ANITA OYAKHILOME

- DON'T PACK YOUR BAGS YET!
- WISDOM FOR WOMEN
- UNENDING SPRING OF JOY

Visit www.christembassy.org

PROPHECY: UNDERSTANDING THE POWER THAT CONTROLS YOUR FUTURE

NEW RELEASE!

Discover from this timely classic by Pastor Chris that you are a product of the prophetic Word, and you can only be established and make advancements in life through the same. Then learn how to take advantage of the powerful gift of prophecy to order the course of your life, and create the future you ought to have.

THE POWER OF TONGUES

Unlock the Power of the Holy Spirit Within You!

In this book, Pastor Chris teaches you the "what," "how" and "why" of speaking in other tongues, and reveals the immense benefits it holds for you as a New Testament believer in Jesus Christ.

HOW TO MAKE YOUR FAITH WORK

Don't get stuck in the rut;
learn how to make your faith work!

In this outstanding masterpiece, Pastor Chris teaches you not just how to acquire faith, but also how to put your faith to work so you can live the life of victory, success, joy, health and, prosperity that God has planned for you.

PRAYING THE RIGHT WAY

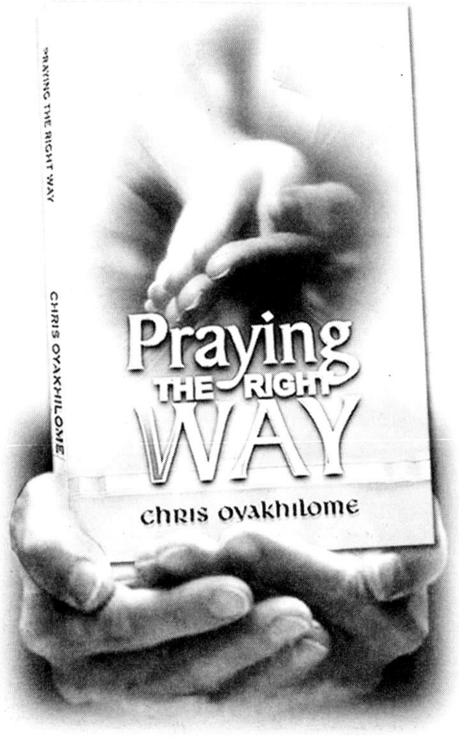

Catch a passion for prayer as you discover the dynamic principles of effective prayer in this book.

The principles are simple, the results guaranteed—a life full of joy and peace as you receive answers to your prayers....always.

DON'T PACK YOUR BAGS YET!

In this riveting piece by Anita Oyakhilome, learn how to change the darkest hours of your life into moments of triumph, as you journey with her in this inspirational classic.

Lord help me to be a light

Beare